Bobcats

by Caroline Arnold
photographs by Richard R. Hewett

Lerner Publications Company • Minneapolis, Minnesota

To Art
  —CA

To Joan, Chris and Angela
          —RRH

Thanks to our series consultant, Sharyn Fenwick, elementary science/math specialist. Mrs. Fenwick was the winner of the National Science Teachers Association 1991 Distinguished Teaching Award. She also was the recipient of the Presidential Award for Excellence in Math and Science Teaching, representing the state of Minnesota at the elementary level in 1992.

Richard R. Hewett's photographs were taken at the Living Desert Wildlife and Botanical Park in Palm Desert, California.

Additional photos are reproduced through the courtesy of: pp. 12, 14, 25, 27, 28, 31-34, 36, 39 © Alan & Sandy Carey; p. 20 © A. Arnold.

Early Bird Nature Books were conceptualized by Ruth Berman and designed by Steve Foley. Series editor is Joelle Goldman.

Text copyright © 1997 by Caroline Arnold
Photographs copyright © 1997 by Richard R. Hewett, except where noted

Library of Congress Cataloging-in-Publication Data

Arnold, Caroline.
    Bobcats / by Caroline Arnold ; photographs by Richard R. Hewett.
      p. cm. – (Early bird nature books)
    Includes index.
    Summary: Describes the life cycle, behavior, and habitat of and dangers faced by bobcats, the stubby-tailed wildcats native to North America.
    ISBN 0-8225-3021-X (alk. paper)
    1. Bobcat—Juvenile literature. [1. Bobcat.] I. Hewett, Richard, ill. II. Title. III. Series.
QL737.C23A748 1997
599.74'428—dc20   96-35084

Manufactured in the United States of America
1 2 3 4 5 6 – SP – 02 01 00 99 98 97

Contents

Alaska (U.S.)

CANADA

N

The bobcat lives in parts of Canada, the United States, and Mexico. The striped areas show exactly where bobcats live.

UNITED STATES

MEXICO

Be a Word Detective

Can you find these words as you read about the bobcat's life? Be a detective and try to figure out what they mean. You can turn to the glossary on page 46 for help.

carnivores	nocturnal	retract
den	nursing	stalking
habitat	predators	territory
litter	prey	tufts

Chapter 1

The bobcat's scientific name is Lynx rufus. How is this wildcat different from a house cat?

Wildcats with Short Tails

As shadows grow long, a small wildcat wakes up from its afternoon nap. Its ears are alert, and its whiskers are twitching. It sniffs the evening air. Soon it will be time to go hunting.

This animal looks much like a house cat. But it is bigger than a house cat. This wildcat has furry tufts at the tips of its ears. And it has a very short tail. It is a bobcat.

The long hairs around the bobcat's head and neck form a collar, or ruff.

Bobcats belong to the cat family. This family is divided into three groups. The big cats are one group. The cheetah is the only member of the second group. The small cats are the third group. The bobcat is one of the small cats.

All of the small cats can purr. The mountain lion is the largest of the small cats. It can weigh up to 200 pounds!

The end of a bobcat's tail has a black stripe across the top and a white tip.

All cats are furry and have claws and sharp teeth. Most cats also have long tails. But the bobcat's tail is just a few inches long. It looks as if someone cut it off, or "bobbed" it. That's how the bobcat got its name.

Bobcats have rough tongues. A bobcat uses its tongue to clean its fur.

A fully grown bobcat is 2 to 4 feet long from its nose to the tip of its tail. It is up to 2 feet tall at the shoulder. A bobcat can weigh up

10

A male bobcat weighs up to 25 pounds. Females usually weigh only about 16 pounds.

to 25 pounds. Male and female bobcats look alike. But males are usually larger than females.

The bobcat looks much like another wildcat, the northern lynx (lingks). But lynxes are bigger than bobcats. Lynxes have longer legs and larger paws.

The northern lynx is also called the Canada lynx. The scientific name of the northern lynx is Lynx canadensis.

The bobcat's thick fur helps keep it warm at night and in cold weather.

A bobcat's fur is usually reddish tan. This color is also called "bay." So the bobcat is sometimes called the bay lynx. Many bobcats have dark streaks or spots on their fur.

Chapter 2

Bobcats often live in places that have many trees. What do we call the kind of place where an animal lives?

Bobcats at Home

Bobcats live in southern Canada, the United States, and Mexico. The kind of place where an animal lives is called its habitat. Bobcats are at home in woods, thickets, swamps, deserts, and mountains.

Bobcats sometimes live near towns. But they are good at hiding. So people rarely see bobcats, even when they are nearby.

Adult bobcats usually live alone. Each bobcat has an area of its own where it lives and hunts. This area is its territory. The size of a bobcat's territory may be less than a square mile. Or it may be as big as 25 square miles.

A bobcat's tan fur matches the color of the dirt and rocks and helps it to hide.

A bobcat can live in a small territory if there is plenty of food. But in some places, there isn't much food. Then a bobcat needs a bigger territory. It needs more room to hunt for food. Besides food, a bobcat's territory must have safe places for sleeping. A bobcat also needs places where it can get out of the rain, wind, and sun.

A shady ledge makes a good place for bobcats to rest.

Bobcats use their teeth and claws to defend themselves.

A bobcat sprays urine on bushes and rocks at the edges of its territory. The smell of the urine says to other bobcats, "Keep out!"

If two bobcats meet, they may fight. But usually bobcats try to keep out of each other's way.

Chapter 3

Bobcats are expert hunters. What kinds of animals do bobcats hunt?

Born to Hunt

Like other cats, bobcats are carnivores (KAHR-nuh-vorz). Carnivores are animals who eat meat. Bobcats get their food by hunting other animals. Animals who hunt for food are called predators (PREH-duh-turz).

The animals that a predator kills are its prey. Bobcats usually hunt rabbits, squirrels, mice, birds, and other small animals. Sometimes bobcats kill larger prey, such as porcupines and deer.

Deer can run fast. Usually, it's hard for a bobcat to catch a deer.

A bobcat must be quick to catch a rabbit or hare.

A bobcat's body helps it to be a good hunter. Its long, strong legs are good for jumping and running. Sharp claws and teeth help a bobcat to kill its prey.

A bobcat uses sharp teeth to grab and hold its prey.

Bobcats have a good sense of balance. They can walk along narrow ledges and climb trees. When they climb, they use their sharp claws to hold on.

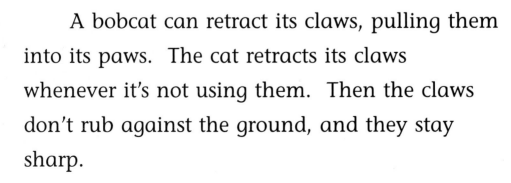

A bobcat scratches trees and logs to keep its claws sharp (right). When a bobcat is not using its claws, it pulls them into its paws (below).

A bobcat can retract its claws, pulling them into its paws. The cat retracts its claws whenever it's not using them. Then the claws don't rub against the ground, and they stay sharp.

Bobcats use their eyes and ears to find prey. A bobcat can easily see a bird's feather fluttering to the ground. And it can see a mouse darting through tall grass. The bobcat listens for the chirping of birds and the squeaking of mice.

A bobcat's soft, padded paws help it to walk quietly.

A bobcat usually hunts by stalking (STAW-king). This means it sneaks up to its prey. The bobcat creeps slowly toward the animal.

Bobcats can run fast, but only for a short distance.
They often hide and wait for prey to come near them.

A bobcat's strong legs help it to pounce on its prey.

Staying low to the ground, the cat hides behind bushes and rocks. Its spotted fur is hard to see in the shadows. And the bobcat is so quiet that its prey does not hear it. The bobcat gets very close to its prey. Then it springs forward. It attacks its prey by surprise.

You might use your hands to feel your way in the dark. A bobcat's whiskers help it to feel its way as it creeps toward its prey.

Animals that are active at night are called nocturnal. Many of the animals that bobcats hunt are nocturnal. These animals are easier to find at night. So bobcats do most of their hunting after dark. They rest during the day. That is why people rarely see them. The bobcats are out hunting when we are asleep. And bobcats are sleeping while we are awake.

Bobcats often hunt mice and other small animals.

It isn't easy to be a predator. Sometimes food is hard to find. And if a predator gets sick or hurt, it cannot hunt. A bobcat can't live without food. In zoos, bobcats are protected.

A bobcat has caught a snowshoe hare. Rabbits and hares are bobcats' favorite food.

After a night of hunting, a bobcat licks its fur clean.

They get plenty of food. They sometimes live as long as 25 years. But wild bobcats have to take care of themselves. So wild bobcats usually don't live as long as bobcats in zoos.

Chapter 4

A small cave is a safe place for a mother bobcat to have her kittens. How much does a newborn bobcat weigh?

Family Life

Most bobcat kittens are born in the spring. Just before a female bobcat is ready to have kittens, she finds a den. The den may be a small cave, a hole in a tree, or a rocky ledge. With her mouth, the mother bobcat carries grass, moss, or leaves to the den. She uses these things to make a soft nest.

A bobcat mother usually has a litter of two or three kittens. Each kitten weighs less than a pound and is covered with short, spotted fur. The kittens' eyes are closed tight. They do not open until the kittens are 9 or 10 days old.

A bobcat family is made up of a mother bobcat and her kittens. This bobcat family lives under a fallen tree.

New bobcat kittens are helpless and hungry. Their mother keeps them warm and clean and safe. She feeds them milk from the teats on her belly. When kittens drink their mother's milk, they are nursing. Bobcat kittens nurse until they are about three months old.

Sometimes a mother bobcat moves her kittens to a new den. She carries them in her mouth, one at a time.

Young bobcat kittens are playful.

Baby bobcats grow quickly. They are soon ready to explore their world. They chase each other and pounce on leaves and insects.

While the kittens play or sleep in the den, their mother goes hunting. She must eat well so she stays strong and healthy. If the mother bobcat gets sick, she won't be able to take care of her kittens.

A mother bobcat takes good care of her kittens.

When the kittens are about three months old, their teeth have grown strong. They are ready to begin eating meat. So their mother brings meat to the den for them. At first, she brings dead animals. Later, she carries live prey to the den. She lets the kittens learn how to catch and kill the prey on their own.

The kittens grow bigger and stronger. Soon they are old enough to leave the den. From then on, they follow their mother. They will not return to the den again.

Even at night, bobcat kittens can see the white spots on the backs of their mother's ears. The spots help the kittens to follow their mother.

The kittens watch their mother as she hunts. They learn how to stalk prey. Later, they begin to hunt by themselves. At first, the young bobcats are clumsy. They make mistakes when they hunt. But they keep practicing. They become experts at catching prey.

As they get older, kittens begin to explore on their own.

When a bobcat kitten grows up, it must leave its mother and find its own territory.

Bobcat kittens stay with their mother until they are about nine months old. By then they are almost fully grown. They can take care of themselves. When the young bobcats are a year old, they will start their own families.

Chapter 5

Great horned owls sometimes hunt young bobcats. What other animals kill bobcats?

Dangers

 Foxes and owls sometimes kill young bobcats. Mountain lions can kill both young and adult bobcats. But usually bobcats can escape from predators. They may be able to run away or climb a tree. If they are cornered, they fight fiercely.

Bobcats climb well. Sometimes they climb trees to get away from danger.

Every year, people kill more than 100,000 bobcats for their fur.

The biggest danger to bobcats is people.
Some people trap bobcats for their fur. And

40

Mice and rats sometimes eat food that people grow.
Bobcats help people by hunting these pests.

some people think bobcats are pests. So they hunt and kill the cats. Bobcats sometimes do kill chickens or other small farm animals. But most of the time bobcats hunt wild animals. Bobcats help people by killing rats and mice.

A bobcat hunts for a mouse in a clump of grass.

You may go camping or hiking where bobcats live. But you probably won't see them. Bobcats sleep during the day, and they are good at hiding. But if you are lucky, you may spy this quick wildcat with its short "bobbed" tail.

Like other cats, a bobcat spends much of its life asleep.

On Sharing a Book

As you know, adults greatly influence a child's attitude toward reading. When a child sees you read, or when you share a book with a child, you're sending a message that reading is important. Show the child that reading a book together is important to you. Find a comfortable, quiet place. Turn off the television and limit other distractions, such as telephone calls.

Be prepared to start slowly. Take turns reading parts of this book. Stop and talk about what you're reading. Talk about the photographs. You may find that much of the shared time is spent discussing just a few pages. This discussion time is valuable for both of you, so don't move through the book too quickly. If the child begins to lose interest, stop reading. Continue sharing the book at another time. When you do pick up the book again, be sure to revisit the parts you have already read. Most importantly, enjoy the book!

Be a Vocabulary Detective

You will find a word list on page 5. Words selected for this list are important to the understanding of the topic of this book. Encourage the child to be a word detective and search for the words as you read the book together. Talk about what the words mean and how they are used in the sentence. Do any of these words have more than one meaning? You will find these words defined in a glossary on page 46.

What about Questions?

Use questions to make sure the child understands the information in this book. Here are some suggestions:

> What did this paragraph tell us? What does this picture show? What do you think we'll learn about next? What things must a bobcat's territory have? Could a bobcat live in your backyard? Why/Why not? How do bobcats get their food? What animals do bobcats hunt? How does a bobcat keep its claws sharp? How is a bobcat family like your family and how is it different? What do you think it's like being a bobcat? What is your favorite part of the book? Why?

If the child has questions, don't hesitate to respond with questions of your own, such as: What do *you* think? Why? What is it that you don't know? If the child can't remember certain facts, turn to the index.

Introducing the Index

The index is an important learning tool. It helps readers get information quickly without searching throughout the whole book. Turn to the index on page 47. Choose an entry, such as *claws,* and ask the child to use the index to find out how bobcats use their claws. Repeat this exercise with as many entries as you like. Ask the child to point out the differences between an index and a glossary. (The index helps readers find information quickly, while the glossary tells readers what words mean.)

Where in the World?

Many plants and animals found in the Early Bird Nature Books series live in parts of the world other than the United States. Encourage the child to find the places mentioned in this book on a world map or globe. Take time to talk about climate, terrain, and how you might live in such places.

All the World in Metric!

Although our monetary system is in metric units (based on multiples of 10), the United States is one of the few countries in the world that does not use the metric system of measurement. Here are some conversion activities you and the child can do using a calculator:

WHEN YOU KNOW:	MULTIPLY BY:	TO FIND:
miles	1.609	kilometers
feet	0.3048	meters
inches	2.54	centimeters
gallons	3.787	liters
tons	0.907	metric tons
pounds	0.454	kilograms

Activities

Make up a story about bobcats. Be sure to include information from this book. Draw or paint pictures to illustrate your story.

Visit a zoo to see several kinds of cats. How are the cats similar to one another, and how are they different?

Pretend you are a bobcat who is waiting quietly for prey to come near. Sit on the ground in your backyard or in a park. Be very quiet. Try not to move your head, arms, or legs. How long can you sit perfectly still? Can you sit still long enough that birds, rabbits, or squirrels will come close to you?

Glossary

carnivores (KAHR-nuh-vorz)—animals who eat flesh or meat

den—a hidden, safe place

habitat—an area where a kind of animal can live and grow

litter—a group of babies born at one time in the same family

nocturnal—active at night

nursing—drinking mother's milk

predators (PREH-duh-turz)—animals who hunt other animals for food

prey—animals who are hunted and eaten by other animals

retract—to pull claws back into the paws. A bobcat retracts its claws when it is not using them.

stalking (STAW-king)—hunting an animal by sneaking up on it

territory—an animal's very own place

tufts—the bunches of dark hair at the tips of a bobcat's ears

Index

Pages listed in **bold** type refer to photographs.

About the Author

Caroline Arnold is the author of more than 100 books for young readers. Her well-received titles include *Cats: In from the Wild, Saving the Peregrine Falcon, A Walk on the Great Barrier Reef,* and *Watching Desert Wildlife,* published by Carolrhoda Books. Since childhood, she has been fascinated with cats, both as pets and in the wild. She grew up in Minneapolis, Minnesota, and studied art at Grinnell College and the University of Iowa. Ms. Arnold lives in Los Angeles, California, where she teaches part-time in the Writers' Program at UCLA Extension.

About the Photographer

Richard R. Hewett was born and raised in St. Paul, Minnesota. He graduated from California's Art Center School of Design with a major in photojournalism. He has illustrated more than 50 children's books and collaborated with Caroline Arnold on the titles *Saving the Peregrine Falcon, Tule Elk,* and *Ostriches and Other Flightless Birds,* published by Carolrhoda Books. Dick and his wife, writer Joan Hewett, live in southern California.